LEADERSHIP JOURNAL

50 Quote Prompts

JOURNALSANDMORE.COM

Want to develop leadership skills? Try journaling. It's an effective, proven method people apply to quotes that inspire you to write about skills you already have and ones you want to develop. there is a quote at the top of each 2 pages to prompt you to write about your experiences and ways you intend to develop better skills. Leadership Journal will help your efforts to do just that.

When it's down on the page, people can examine their thoughts with more rationality. A journal is a safe place to express honest thoughts and emotions without the risk of judgment from others. It is a way people find that inner part of their soul emerging to guide them and give them the answers them didn't think they had. They'll begin to understand why quotes can inspire you to reflect on your own skills, or motivate you to develop better leadership for others, as well as uncover inner strength and leadership skills that can help you professionally.

We all know seeking to develop those inate leadership skills is beneficial in succeeding in today's fast paced job market. It is challenging and everyone will develop leadership skills at their own pace.

This journal will leave anyone:

- Planning activities around what has happened in the past.

- Having a place to make relevant notes about your performance

- Logging your leadership development progress.

Whether someone wants to have the skills to succeed. or develops those inner leadership skills, this journal is the first step to develop leadership skills. Get this book today and get started right now.

Aleader is one who knows the way, goes the way, and shows the way. John C. Maxwell

Agenuine leader is not a searcher for consensus but a molder of consensus. Martin Luther King, Jr.

If your actions inspire others to dream more, learn more, do more and become more, you are a leader.
John Quincy Adams

Innovation distinguishes between a leader and a follower.
Steve Jobs

People ask the difference between a leader and a boss. The leader leads, and the boss drives. Theodore Roosevelt

No man will make a great leader who wants to do it all himself or get all the credit for doing it. Andrew Carnegie

A good leader takes a little more than his share of the blame, a little less than his share of the credit. Arnold H. Glasow

The task of the leader is to get his people from where they are to where they have not been. Henry A. Kissinger

The art of communication is the language of leadership.
James Humes

The quality of a leader is reflected in the standards
they set for themselves. Ray Kroc

Leadership and learning are indispensable to each other.
John F. Kennedy

Leadership is the capacity to translate vision into reality. Warren Bennis

The task of leadership is not to put greatness into humanity, but to elicit it, for the greatness is already there. John Buchan

Leadership cannot really be taught. It can only be learned. Harold S. Geneen

Leadership is getting someone to do what they don't want to do, to achieve what they want to achieve. Tom Landry

Leadership is unlocking people's potential to become
better. Bill Bradley

Leadership consists of picking good men and helping them do their best. Chester W. Nimitz

Without initiative, leaders are simply workers in leadership positions. Bo Bennett

Management is doing things right

leadership is doing the right things. Peter Drucker

The key to successful leadership today is influence, not authority. Ken Blanchard

Leadership is the art of getting someone else to do something you want done because he wants to do it.
Dwight D. Eisenhower

Effective leadership is not about making speeches or being liked

leadership is defined by results not attributes. Peter
Drucker

Leaders must be close enough to relate to others, but far enough ahead to motivate them. John C. Maxwell

The function of leadership is to produce more leaders, not more followers. Ralph Nader

Leadership is an opportunity to serve. It is not a
trumpet call to self-importance. J. Donald Walters

Leadership is a way of thinking, a way of acting and, most importantly, a way of communicating. Simon Sinek

Leadership is practiced not so much in words as in attitude and in actions. Harold S. Geneen

Aleader does not deserve the name unless he is willing occasionally to stand alone. Henry A. Kissinger

Leadership is the key to 99 percent of all successful efforts. Erskine Bowles

Leadership appears to be the art of getting others to want to do something you are convinced should be done. Vance Packard

Become the kind of leader that people would follow voluntarily

even if you had no title or position. Brian Tracy

The real leader has no need to lead - he is content to point the way. Henry Miller

Leadership comes in small acts as well as bold strokes.
Carly Fiorina

Real leadership is leaders recognizing that they serve the people that they lead. Pete Hoekstra

Leadership means forming a team and working toward common objectives that are tied to time, metrics, and resources. Russel Honore

Leadership is about vision and responsibility, not power.
Seth Berkley

Leadership is intangible, and therefore no weapon ever designed can replace it. Omar N.Bradley

Leadership offers an opportunity to make a difference in someone's life, no matter what the project. Bill Owens

True leadership isn't about having an idea. It's about having an idea and recruiting other people to execute on this vision. Leila Janah

Aleader is best when people barely know he exists, when his work is done, his aim fulfilled, they will say: we did it ourselves. Lao Tzu

You don't lead by pointing and telling people some place to go. You lead by going to that place and making a case.
Ken Kesey

Agreat leader's courage to fulfill his vision comes from passion, not position. John Maxwell

Aman who wants to lead the orchestra must turn his back on the crowd. Max Lucado

Great leaders are not defined by the absence of weakness, but rather by the presence of clear strengths. John Zenger

Leaders conceive and articulate goals that lift people out of their petty preoccupations and unite them in pursuit of objectives worthy of their best efforts

John Gardener

Leadership does not always wear the harness of compromise. Woodrow Wilson

One of the tests of leadership is the ability to recognize a problem before it becomes an emergency. Arnold Glasow

The final test of a leader is that he leaves behind him in other men, the conviction and the will to carry on.

Walter Lippman

The greatest leaders mobilize others by coalescing people around a shared vision. Ken Blanchard

Made in the USA
Columbia, SC
10 December 2020